CATCH YERSELF ON!

CATCH YERSELF ON!

John Pepper

Illustrations by Rowel Friers.

Blackstaff Press

Also by John Pepper

A Quare Geg
See Me, See Her
What a Thing to Say

First published in 1980
by The Blackstaff Press Limited
3 Galway Park, Dundonald, Belfast BT16 0AN
and
27 South Main Street, Wolfeboro, New Hampshire 03894 USA

Reprinted in 1981, 1982, 1984, 1985, 1987

Printed in Northern Ireland
by Belfast Litho Printers Limited
ISBN 0-85640-237-0

Contents

Far be it from me

You are stopped in the street by a stranger who says conversationally, 'A friend of mine told me yesterday, "The last time I saw my cousin Paul he was waiting in the Casuality Department dressed to kill'."

You are in a supermarket check-out queue and hear the woman in front of you say to her companion, 'If that motorist had hit me that was my inside away with the band again.'

You open a letter and read, 'The woman next door said to me "I could cry with my feet so I could."'

Your telephone rings and the caller asks, 'Did you hear of the woman who went into a chemist's and said, "Awant some waddin' for meers."?'

You are in a bus and the woman in the seat in front says to the girl beside her, 'The man ast me where Durm Street was an' I said "Stray ton, cudden mist" and he lucked at me as if I was daft.'

I would be straining credulity by suggesting that these are the kind of things that only happen in Northern Ireland. The point is they have happened to me — and keep happening.

On each occasion I am convinced afresh that the foibles and eccentricities of the Ulster idiom have unique qualities, qualities that set them apart, whatever may be their root cause.

If in the following pages I leave myself open to the charge that I am only going over well-tilled ground, my answer is that it it is fruitful ground. And it is ground capable of providing many rich crops, each one different to the one before.

Language, whatever its form, whatever the accent used, is never static. It is forever changing, forever being renewed. It is as full of divergence as the people who use it, as inexhaustible as human nature itself.

This, then, is my reason for once more treading the fascinating paths that enable me to share my delight in the extraordinary things people say in

Northern Ireland and the way they say them.

Other communities have no less singular idiomatic qualities but those to be encountered in Ulster can hold their own with any of them.

It is said of showbiz that it isn't what you do but how you do it. In Ulster it is not what you say but how you say it.

The lady who could cry with her feet surely deserves some degree of immortality, even if it is only on a printed page.

Once more I put on record my deep sense of gratitude to the people who act as eavesdroppers and tell me of the infinite curiosities of speech they have heard. I owe them a considerable debt.

Shizawed, issent she?

Language purists may well shudder each time they hear Belfast speech at its most uninhibited. Nevertheless it has its own special characteristics. It may not always be easily understood but it has heart and it has backbone. The fact remains that if the pedants had their way the results might not be what they expect.

Were they to dominate, everyday conversation would be left without life. It might be precise but it would certainly lack the colour of this piece of dialogue between two women in a Belfast bus:

'Still livin' in Cornelia Street?'

'Am.'

'Still likin' it?'

'Am.'

'Goin' home ni?'

'Am.'

'Still stickin' it out wi' yir man?'

'Am.'

'Sloggin' away in the same oul' place?'

'Am.'

'Goin' away for the Twalfth?'

'Am.'

'Stayin' at the same oul' place?'

'Am.'

Some may call it ham-fisted chit-chat, a description which could be confirmed when the less taciturn of the two ladies was later heard showing a strong attachment for the expression 'Soam' to indicate her resolved to take a particular line of action:

'I'm goin' to tell him straight, soam. I'm goin' to tell him this very night, soam. I'm sick sore and tired of the way he behaves till me, soam. I'm goin' to have it out with him, soam.'

It could all be called Ulster's 'morr tung'. Certainly the evidence of its persistent use is overwhelming. The air is filled with it.

And the air is all the more lively for it; all the more stimulating, as in:

'Ar Maudie's workin' again.'

'Shizzent.'

'Shiz.'

'Honest?'

'Shiz. Sure enough.'

'Shizawed anyway, issent she?'·

'Right enough. Shizawed. She wis awed from the first day she opened her bake.'

Soon after one of the women was heard to insist, 'It's a pity of her. She was great value.' Whether or not the 'odd' Maudie was meant, and how considerable her 'value' was, will never be known.

A mention is thoroughly earned by the woman who said she was 'suffering from retired husband' and I listened carefully for the symptoms of this unusual complaint. They duly came:

'I'm kilt lookin' after him. Parritch for his breakfast. He's mad about his parritch. Bovril at alavan. Spuds for his dinner at wan. A boiled egg for his tay besides the toast. He goes through the toast like a cyclone. Then tay again at bedtime an' yir life's not worth livin' if you haven't the cream crackers to go with it. I'm cookin' an' washin' after him from morn till night. I'm wore out, soam.'

There are rich rewards for listening carefully to the snatches of conversation in the shopping queue, in the street, as well as in the bus.

A woman who had a small boy beside her in a bus kept long-sufferingly answering his insistent questions during the journey. The boy understood her explanations. Not everyone else would have felt they were in the picture.

He had spotted: (a) a donkey, (b) a large dog, (c) a bicycle that had fallen over on the pavement, (d) a three-wheeled motor car, (e) a man with an umbrella blown inside out, and (f) an Orange decoration stretching across the road.

All her answers were to the point. They were:

(a) 'Sanass'

(b) 'Sadawg.'

(c) 'Sabisleek.'

(d) 'Sacar.'

(e) 'Sanijit.'

(f) 'Sanarch.'

But 'morr tung' is not confined to the ladies. Male exponents are easy to come by, introducing their own refinements, as in:

'Sammyboy. Howsaboutye?'

'Ack. Rightly, Jimmy.'

'Still graftin'?'

'Nathin' else forrit.'

'What about the wee wumman?'

'Ack, she's lyin' wi' the dacter. She's up the chute and y'know the way her oul' pressure always rises. Breathe on her and begod it's riz.'

'Ack, A'm sarry, Sammy. It'll put the knockers on the oul' soff-shoe shufflin' and the competitions comin' aff.'

'Ack, she wudden a went anyway. Sure she nivver had no feet for it. 'Sages since I got her to a dance.'

'Pity, Sammy.'

'Right enuf. Still, 'slife, issent it?'

''Slife all right, Sammy.'

The verbal short cuts involved when 'morr tung' is used in Ulster reach remarkable lengths.

It is difficult not to feel sorry for the small boy of whom it was said: 'He's not well. Never slep the whole night. It's the bile. He's been atin' hips an' haws an' I'm keepin' him in his bed. They say congestion is infectious. I don't know where to turn.'

Then she added, 'As if that wasn't bad enough. In the middle of it all the cat was as sick as a dog.'

Lexicographers would find Northern Ireland a rich treasure-house.

There are the asides in the supermarket check-out queues like:

'He dove aff up the six-fut springboard and I div in after him.'

'I nivver bake ni. It only gets ate.'

'They divid the apple cake down the middle.'

'I don't usually wear trousers so often but this winter I haven't had them aff my back.'

When people start telling you about a friend who has become a 'cause girl' caution is called for. Not everyone will know in a flash that the young lady has won a job in the chorus.

The shopper in Belfast city centre who was heard telling a companion, 'Sin here' wasn't involved in an exhortation to break one of the Commandments. It was just her way of saying, 'This is the shop where I saw the skirt I was telling you about.'

Nor had the girl who told a friend, 'Mon moan' lapsed into O-level French. She was indicating that she was unaccompanied.

The woman in a public library who replied 'frew dunt' when asked what

10

she was looking for was in search of a crime story.

And the mother who was heard telling her small son as he was about to tackle a lollipop, 'Liar intit' wasn't actually swearing at the child, merely using the colloquialism, 'Leather into it.'

To ask in an Ulster newsagent's for a 'day mare' ensures that you are handed the Daily Mirror, while the news that you want 'bare chews' means nothing more than a resolve to buy new footwear.

A diner in a Montreal restaurant heard this conversation going on in an adjoining booth:

'I always go there,' said one speaker.

'Aye sodayi,' said another.

A third speaker then said, 'Sodayi.'

The listener put his head round and said, 'Aye, an sodayi.'

There was a moment's startled pause before the question came simultaneously from the trio: 'Wherreryefrim?'

The man who had been listening came from Newtownards. The trio came respectively from the Shankill Road, the Woodstock Road, and Newtownabbey.

From that moment they ceased to be strangers.

A fringe snookers ye for wearin' a hat.'

Those who find difficulty in appreciating the variety of uses to which the spoken word is put in Ulster may sometimes get the idea that a deliberate effort is made to be ambigious. This is not so. If confusion is caused it is not intentional.

The woman, for example, who was asked where she got the glasses she was wearing and answered, 'I got them from a dentist on the Antrim Road' isn't setting out to perplex her questioner. She is simply making what she considers to be a statement of fact. She is positive it was a dentist, even if it was almost certainly an optician.

She would ask the question, 'How long do I have to stay in bed till I get up?' in the same disarming manner, oblivious to any bewilderment she might cause.

The statement 'I haven't my teeth in and I'm talking upside down' applies to many pronouncements quite unrelated to the absence of dentures.

A woman explained to the milkman seeking payment of his account, 'I told the wee lad to tell you I'd see you next week an' my man's not workin' and my head's no better.'

The same approach was made by the lady who said, 'I wasn't dressed and

I was just beginning to put on the porridge when there was a knock at the door. I was fairly put on.'

Delays caused by a stubborn tenant to a big rebuilding project were put in their proper perspective by the statement, 'I know the woman well. Wee Mrs McConkey. She's living in a condemned street and damn the budge will she make. It's her that's holding up the pulling down.'

There is a special quality about the grumble, 'I ast her to keep a watch for the postman and she wanted to know if it mattered if it wasn't a self winder.'

Constantly the impression is created that the speakers live in a mad world. Once this is accepted everything becomes clear.

A public library assistant was asked if it would be possible to borrow a book about the Salvation Army. The enquirer said a friend had read it and said it was very good.

It took several minutes' probing before it was established that what was wanted was A. J. Cronin's *The Citadel*.

The complaint 'A fringe fairly snookers ye for wearing a hat' calls for a feminine understanding of hair styles to be really appreciated.

'She's the girl that wears the brown coat that comes to the door' and 'The wages is ridiculous but the money's good' are also the kind of statements not instantly grasped if you don't pay attention.

So too is the request made by an elderly woman in a furniture store, 'I'm lookin' for a wee bit of carpet for my back passage. Could I see what you've got?'

A restaurant waitress new to the job had problems in concealing her surprise when a diner was asked is she would have a sweet, and was told, 'No but I'll have a wee knowin' of cheese just to taste my mouth.'

It isn't often that a tribute to someone's talent will take the form of the statement, 'He's a great musician. You should see him fiddling with his moustache.'

The eccentricities are endless. There was the tenant who was asked if he could recommend to a neighbour the type of back boiler he used.

'Man I could,' was the reply. 'With a heart and a half. Sure the hot water in this house is never cold. You couldn't ask any more than that.'

It is a safe bet that the same man, criticising a soccer goal which had been re-run on television, said, 'Sure there was nathin' great about that. He done it in slow motion.'

The same approach to enlightenment was made by a woman who was having her roof insulated. One of the workmen brought his little girl along to lend a hand.

As the work was going on she appeared rubbing her wrist, saying, 'This is

'He's a great musician. You should see him fiddling with his moustache.'

terrible stuff to work with. He's up there scratchin' himself to death. You'd think he was livin'.'

Even in seeking enlightenment trouble can arise. A woman went into a corner shop in Belfast (obviously one of those customers who expect the people behind the counter to work miracles) and announced: 'Can you do anything about it? The picture on me wireless has gone.'

It is easy to appreciate the perplexity of the manager of a new factory, a German who was learning English. He was faced by an employee who complained to him that the supervisor was rude:

'In what way was he rude?' the worker was asked.

'He just ates the face off you.'

'What does that mean?' said the manager. 'Explain.'

'He can't speak to you without jumpin' down your throat.'

'But nobody could do that.'

'Well he can. He's always chewin' the rag.'

At this stage, the poor manager gave up the struggle.

'Just folly the telegraft poles.'

Those who seek to denigrate Ulster's vernacular, denounce it as largely incomprehensible, and write off all who use it as inarticulate eccentrics, are not really doing the Province justice.

The truth is that dialectal idiocies are universal. No area is immune from them.

Who can argue that there s a basic difference between the Australian who says he liked 'baked necks' for breakfast when he means bacon and eggs, and the Ulsterman who orders a meal of 'staken ships', when his sights are set on sirloin and French-fries?

It is well known that a Strine, checking the price of an article, will enquire 'Emma Chissett?' An Ulsterman on a similar quest will ask, 'Musherye lukin'?'

Canadians will tell you they live in Oddawa (although there are times when it could be either Tronno or Trannah) and a North of Ireland native will speak of belonging to Dari or Banker, when the places meant are Ottawa, Toronto, Derry and Bangor respectively.

It is a nice question whether a woman's request in an Ulster accent in a New York store for a 'nammel mug' would be easily understood. In Belfast it would be instantly known what a 'linn short' is, provided it was looked for in a men's outfitters.

The tourist from Lisburn who went into a shop in Leeds, with a small boy at her heels, and was continually interrupted by his plea 'Biasabunma' would be apt to create the impression that foreigners had arrived.

But is the youngster's style of seeking a currant bun any more open to indictment than the Yorkshire woman's, 'That skirt's fouty', meaning it is badly made?

A character in a Western will declare 'Ingonna' to indicate a resolve not to take some specific action. In Ulster such a statement would take the form of 'Naawalnat.'

If a Dubliner says he comes from Sullen Iron it is nothing more than a vocal oddity little different from the Co Down man's disclosure that he was born in Car Door. The references are of course to Southern Ireland and Carrowdore.

A store in Brisbane was flummoxed by a request for an 'egg nisher', otherwise an air cooler. The confusion was comparable to that in a Shankill Road shop when a small boy asked for 'a blaka ribble'. What he had in his sights was a block of ripple ice cream.

The point about all these examples is that each is in exactly the same mould. Each speaker is exercising the local right to say something in the way he expects his hearers will understand. They, not he, are at fault if they don't.

More than once I have been reproached for drawing attention to our speech foibles. 'It is surely a grave reflection on the Province to publicise such revolting examples of jarring, uncultured speech as ''Seeya'' when ''I am now leaving'' is meant,' ran one indictment.

I do not agree. Verbal eccentricities are universal. Language would lose a great deal of its liveliness without them.

The Tyke version of 'There is something wrong' takes the form of 'Summatsupeer' yet it should not necessarily be dismissed as an uncouth utterance.

Nor should the Newtownards Road man's enquiry 'Wassup?' In each case the person addressed understands what is meant. That is surely what matters.

Geordie is a speech style with deviations completely acceptable in Newcastle-upon-Tyne. If someone say in a bar, 'Gezashort', a small whisky will be served. The Belfast equivalent is 'Givvusahaffin.'

In Yorkshire 'Issegone?' seeks to establish if a guest has taken his leave. In Northern Ireland a similar enquiry would take the form of 'Asse lef?'

Few things are more guaranteed to create the impression that local speech is highly individualistic than the answers given to the visitor who asks the way. One tourist found it so entertaining to listen to local advice that he often made the enquiry quite unnecessarily.

One of the gems of his collection ran 'Gwan on ahead till ye cum to the first loanin' on yir right haun an' turn the corner.'

'Loanin?' asked the visitor. 'What's a loanin'?'

'Ach, it's a wee rough road with high hedges and no signpost.'

No less explicit were the instructions he was given when he stopped in a Co Londonderry village and enquired how far he was from the nearest town.

'Ye'll hae t' turn the kyar roun' an' go down to the bottom of the hill there an' tak th' road that lies t' yir leff. Then if ye just folly the telegraft poles ye'll get there soon enough.'

Who could find fault with advice like that?

Another tourist was told, 'You turn left when you reach the cross-roads. Right? Then turn left again. Right? Then you take the second turning on your left. Right? That's three lefts.'

'Thanks very much,' said the tourist.

'That's all right.'

A native once said to me 'Ya hafta reckanise that we're blingle,' seeking to emphasise in his own droll style that the standard English as used by most people in the Province and the vernacular sometimes resorted to by a great number of them are poles apart.

It is invaluable to know this. If the stranger is armed with the knowledge that the inhabitants are bilingual it will open his eyes. If he tries to ignore it he will suffer the same deprivation as a viction of acute myopia studying a Turner sunset.

It will give him a definite edge to know that when someone says to him, 'Gawn yowlcodye' in an amused tone the speaker has not suddenly swung into Mongolian. It is just that the tolerant warning is being given, 'You're pulling my leg, aren't you?'

It will add immensely to the enjoyment of his visit if he is aware that the statement 'He was crying bitterly' is given added punch if it becomes 'He was cryin' buckets.'

'Who's there? 'Sony me.'

It often strikes me as surprising that, while guide books provide a wealth of detail about the scenic and geographic abnormalities of an area, so little attention is paid to its language peculiarities.

The words and expressions to be encountered only there can be as fascinating a feature of the surroundings as the height of the mountains, the direction of the prevailing winds, the extent of the rainfall.

Not long ago a journalist in the *Guardian* wrote of the pleasure he found in 'listening to Northern Irish speech'.

'Unlike most of the southern lilts which tend to sound whimsical and hesitant the Ulster voice is vigorous and assertive,' he said, and went on to describe an encounter with a small boy who was playing skimmers across the Lagan.

'Mister,' the boy told him, 'this is deadly crack.'

What he meant was 'this is fantastic fun', to the journalist a colourful use of language.

It is an aspect of Ulster life which must be just as interesting as specifying the number of stones on Giant's Causeway, yet guide book writers usually steer clear of any reference to it. It means that the visitor often fails to realise what he is missing.

A chief delight of the Ulster Folk Museum is the extensive collection of tapes of dialect speakers collected by the Museum's researchers. It is an arsenal of surprises.

One is of a Cullybackey man reciting in his homespun tones Shakespeare's 'Seven Ages of Man'.

He follows the script word for word until his rich Co Antrim voice reaches the last line, 'Sans hair, sans teeth, sans eyes, sans everything.'

Here he departs from the original. His version runs 'Nae hair, nae teeth, nae eyes, nae nathin'.'

Devoted Shakespeareans may question his right to take such a liberty. Few Ulstermen would suggest for a moment that an extra dimension had not been added to the original.

It makes a difference, when hearing an order in a cafe for 'Toosh uppers', to appreciate that it is a request for a double helping of fish and chips.

If the visitor thanks someone for telling him the way and gets the reply 'Neighbour' is is an advantage to realise that what is meant is that it was really no bother to be helpful.

17

There is a pleasure of its own to discover for yourself that 'Weel gup ni' is not a phrase in Sanskrit but an intimation that all is ready for going up the stairs.

President Carter was able to speak of 'the awl crisis'. If the White House can get away with a phrase like that who is to deny the right of the Ulsterman to say 'Stew' when his message is that the time has come to pay the electricity bill?

The suggestion has been made that the Ulster face has an influence on Ulster speech. A jutting lip is a common feature of the Northern Ireland look. This, it is argued, is responsible for the oversounding of consonants.

Margaret is turned into Morgit, elastic into elaskit, Ahoghill is pronounced Achle.

A party of Belfast young people on a tour of Holland had their Dutch guide guessing to such an extent that he turned to the leader of the group and said, 'Could you possibly tell me what ''anorn'' means? I don't seem to have heard the word before.'

'Why do you ask?' came the enquiry.

'It's like this,' he explained, 'Every time we come to a windmill one of the boys keeps pointing to it and exclaiming ''There's anorn.'' '

A useful gide to one pronunciation quirk is provided by the lines

As you cross over Derry bridge
You'll see nothing half as grand
As the Channel fleet that ploughs the deep
From Derry to Strabane.

Making Strabane rhyme with grand is not a case of poetic licence. They do scan in the local dialect, as do Bann and band, man and hand, sand and pan.

The owner of a French hotel who prided himself on his fluency in English because of his constant contact with UK guests asked a Northern Ireland visitor if he had slept well.

'Man dear it was well intil the night before I fell over so it was.'

It brought home to the hotelier that there were still some gaps in his lexicon.

The speech variations are multitudinous.

The will take the form of the reply to the question 'Who's there?' which ran ''Sony me.'

Or the advice given by a neighbour to a woman who said, 'I've just foun' a big hole under my sink.'

'Why don't you get the sanity to come out and look into it?' she was told.

A visitor who had to call in bewilderment for a translation was a St John's

Ambulance examiner who was putting candidates through an oral test for their first aid certificates.

It was his first time in Belfast and one of the questions was, 'You find a man unconscious. You would you test to see if he was dead, had fainted, or had been knocked unconscious?'

One candidate elected to deal with the fainting first and said, 'If he had fainted I could see the cowl swate breakin' on him.'

When it was patiently pointed out that 'cold sweat' was in the candidate's mind the examiner returned to English-speaking Wimbledon with a new concept of language.

'Ar grocer hasn't an ounce.'

Ulster people have a talent for producing words that seem almost to have been invented for the occasion.

During a Co Antrim flute band practice the conductor reached the stage of voicing his despair that the perfection he sought could ever be achieved. 'Yir nathin' but a lock av dunnerheaded ramelgerries wae nae rhyme or reason at a'. That's what ye hev me thinkin'.'

The Co Fermanagh man who threatened 'Next time I see that wee targe I'll give her a good joinin''' would leave many people baffled. Except, possibly, his intended victim.

A Co Down man whose car refused to start told a friend, 'Ah lucked her over like an oul' woman luckin' for nits in a wain's head and then a gae her a dunt but she just gae a wee wheezle an' conked out. Ah was fair grieved.'

A father and son were sitting together in a bus when an elegantly dressed woman got on.

'Luck at that burd, farr,' whispered the son. 'Wudden mine her.'

'Son,' said the father, 'when it comes till wimmen ye're a sair glunterpake. Can y' no' see it's just an oul' hen wi' a pullet's head. Are ye bline?'

There is a world of difference in Ulster between, 'I gave her a wee cuddle' and 'I give her a wee hoult.'

A visitor once made the complaint, 'Ulster people are not good conversationalists, their talk being limited to the weather, high prices, and tittle tattle.'

One indignant reaction to the taunt was 'Ah well, there's gran' talk an' a hard hat an' ma head wasn't made for either.'

The impeachment is much too general. There is little evidence that Ulster people are basically taciturn. Prone to frequent attacks of logorrhoea they are not.

A Co Tyrone woman was quoted to me as having said of a neighbour, 'Look at her. She thinks she's somebody and her wi' a turtle hanging.' The reference was to a thread dangling from the hem of her skirt.

An Ontario judge made it known that he wanted a housekeeper to take the place of the Ulsterwoman holding the post who was leaving to be married. He insisted that her successor should have an Ulster accent. Clearly the woman who held the post wasn't only efficient at the job but reached a high degree of acceptablility when she opened her mouth.

A Belfastwoman applied and was duly chosen. Unfortunately nothing is known of the tests she went throught before being appointed. What would the judge have considered to be suitable Ulster sentences?

Possibly she earned ten out of ten if asked, 'Would you mind a great deal if you had to leave Belfast?' by answering 'Ach, A'm fed up with ar grocer. The man hasn't an ounce.'

If she let it slip, 'It only happened to me the wance' would she win a place on the short list?

It could well be that it could have clinched matters for the applicant to be in a position to tell of the Ulster businessman whose secretary was convinced her services were grossly undervalued.

She decided on her own version of industrial action by working to rule and typing every word he said when dictating, grammatical or not. He was a hardware merchant and her first piece of action was on a letter which, in normal circumstances, would have run:

> Dear Sir,
>
> We have been very disappointed at the quality of the consignment of saws we received from you yesterday. At least two dozen of them were flawed. A number of them had clear signs of rust. All are definitely unsaleable and we cannot be expected to pay for them.
>
> In the meantime we are holding them at our premises so that you can come and inspect them.
>
> > Yours faithfully,

This was the secretary's version:

> Dear Thingy,
>
> Ach, tell the oul ijits we take a poor bloody view of the sauce they sowl us. Coupla dozen av them an' there was floss on ivvery wan. They were all rusty. I was sick to my stummick when they were tuk outa the peckin' case. Tell thim that. Watta thowl chancers over there take us fir?
>
> Tell them they hev anor think cummin if they have the notion that we're payin' good money for a bunch of useless oul' sauce. Tell them

we didden cum in on a loda hay. They're losin' their baps if they think that's the way we do business. Tell thim till cum in an' luck at thim an' see for theirselves.

Right m'girl?

'I'll go an' see thowlants.'

Anyone unfamiliar with the deviations of Northern Ireland speech can expect exactly the same problems as a statement in Bantu or Genoaese would cause to those to whom those languages are incomprehensible.

They will be confronted with precisely the same difficulty in demonstrating that they don't understand without making themselves look stupid.

The only alternative to a puzzled 'What was that you said?' or an incredulous 'Eh?' is to nod vaguely as if all was clear.

Either way it is difficult to avoid creating the impression that their ignorance of English is abysmal. It is one of the penalties of being a stranger in Ulster.

Take the comment on a golf course about a player whose skill at the game left much to be desired, 'I played with him last week and he tuk a savan at the secan', anorr savan at the twalfth, and yit anorr savan at the savanteenth. Wasn't that a geg? An' them were his best holes.'

In other words for three holes alone the unfortunate player took twenty-one strokes. If he was correspondingly bad at the others, golf obviously wasn't his game. It was more likely to be cricket.

The safest reply if things are not quite clear is 'Oh!'

A husband told a friend bitterly, 'Shilitonme,' was not using the Urdu word. It is the man's description of the reception he received when he arrived home, 'the worse for the wear,' as he put it.

A Belfastman, staring out of his kitchen window, will call out, 'Sawn', and everyone withing earshot will understand clearly. Only a stranger will fail to appreciate that he is conveying the news that it has started raining.

Anyone fortunate enough not to have to call for a translation will understand perfectly if the next exclamation from the man at the window is 'Soneyaweeshire.' This indicates that all that has happened is that a light shower is falling.

Should the weather be unduly severe this will be shown by the word 'Steemin'' but if the rain is really at its worst the expression used is 'Spoarin''.

If it is the height of summer and the day more like winter the comment is

21

'Spoarin'.

liable to be 'It isn't this time of the year at all.'

A visitor should be careful to nod understandingly if the weather observer announces, 'It'll be dry if it doesn't rain.' It is equally tactful to show a similar reaction if told 'If it keeps up it'll be dry.'

The pitfalls for which a guest should keep a look out don't end there.

If his hostess proposes to go visiting and says, 'I think I'll go and see thowlants', he will be in trouble if he assumes that a trip to one of the local sights is planned. What is intended is a call on her elderly aunts.

Once this 'Norn Iron' tendency is realised the way is made clear for a much greater understanding of the people. References to 'Thowlman', 'Thowlwoman', 'Thowlfella' and 'Thowlbeck' will cease to bewilder. Even 'Thowlfeet' will be comprehended.

Should a discussion arise involving a relation not noted for his generosity, who is nevertheless not a bad sort, it will be tolerantly said of him 'Givvemisjew.'

If the guest is taken along to a party he will miss out if he is unaware of the common method of indicating that he would welcome 'the other half'. This is done by murmuring 'Sempy'. The Ulster host who doesn't recognise the expression doesn't exist.

Introductions can have their tricky moments. If the visitor is faced by a complete stranger and all that is said of him is 'Jinnomabror?' his best bet is to smile and put out his hand. Experience will teach him that he is being introduced to his host's brother.

If his hostess should excuse herself from some of the engagements planned for the following day she does so by saying 'Amgettinmaherrdun'. This is not an expression intended for 'Call my Bluff'. It announces that she has an appointment with her hairdresser.

Should she go to the front door and call out 'Cummeerawantye', her aim is to fetch her small son who has been playing in the street.

If in conversation she exclaims 'Squarendeer' she is not imitating a Teheran bus conductor calling out the next stop. It conveys her certainty that an article she has seen advertised is much too costly.

When the guest is asked what time he would like to be wakened for breakfast, and wants to be on the move around eight o'clock, he will show that he is well on the way to a mastery of the technique of communication in Ulster if he says simply, 'Callusstate'.

Getting the hang of 'Norn Iron' is not by any means as difficult as it would seem. 'Shin?' seeks to establish if someone is at home. 'Shout' aims to discover the same thing, just as 'Shup?' indicates a desire to find if she is up out of her bed.

Nothing could be simpler.

'That fella makes my stummick turn.'

Many Ulster people cherish a strong attachment to the value of an appropriate overture to what they have to say. It is considered important to signal that you have a message. Such indicators as:

'You'll not believe a word of it but...'

'Know what I'm going to tell you...'

'You'll think i'm jokin' but...'

'Lissen a minnit till you hear this...'

'You're never going to credit it...'

All are little more than personalised variations of the town crier's traditional call for attention, 'Oyez, Oyez.'

In each case the aim is the same — to ensure an audience.

'Didya ever hear the like of it?' is invaluable as an introduction to the revelation: 'He brought out a wad of notes that would have stuffed a donkey.'

'Know this?' a woman will say, confident that the bait will be irresistible, and then add, 'My man toul' me he was tired. "Tired!" I said. "What in the name of God would make ye tired? Ye must have dreamt ye were workin'."'

'Far be it from me' has become a popular opener, a fairly mild example of its use being 'Far be it from me but that fella makes my stummick turn.' Others are:

'Far be it from me but that woman of his has a face that would put a mare off its oats.'

'Far be it from me but I was in the optician's when she walked in and said she wanted a pair of sunglasses for her head was jumpin'.'

Devotees of the vogue will pop up in supermarket check-out queues, on the bus, at the corner shop, in doctors' waiting rooms, in cafes, at Post Office pension counters.

It can introduce a snide comment about an unpopular neighbour, a gossipy tit-bit about someone going through a particularly prosperous spell, an aside about someone who has developed superior airs because all goes well for her.

A typical far-be-it-from-me situation developed in the course of an encounter between two friends at a bus stop.

'I see Lizzie has new teeth in.'

'Aye, I run into her and she said her man was only after payin' £100 to let her have her teeth in private. I just said to her, 'Far be it from me,' I said, 'but I minded the time he hadn't a penny to bless hisself with an' he wasn't the one to hand out £100 for I mind him knockin' them down your throat many's the time.'' '

The far-be it-from-me ploy can be adapted to the most harmless pronouncements, as well as the most pungent.

'Far be it from me but I heard Mrs Hardy say right out, "If you don't keep your eyes on your tongue you'll get my hand across your bake.'' '

'Far be it from me but there we were having wir tea when she cum rushin' in threw the dure an' said ''Lettus luk at yir tele quick. I sent Mrs Quigley a Get Well card and I wanta see if her name's in the Deaths Column yet''.'

Another example comes from Dungannon. 'Far be it from me but she said she was takin' aff her when there was a rap at the door. An' there was the coalman wi' a bagga coal.'

Worth a mention is 'Far be it from me but that fella cudden open a tin of sardines without breakin' into a swate,' and 'Far be it from me but that daughter of hers is a targe. She toul' her ma she wanted one of them short skirts and you'd have said to yerself that all she was wearin' was a pelmet.'

It is a usage with its own subtleties. It can be resorted to to introduce a note of caution about the news to follow. It serves to emphasise that the speaker is not one to make rash statements but exercises a degree of prudence before daring to repeat what someone else has said.

'Far be it from me but you'd need a poultice to draw that woman,' indicate the difficulty to be encountered in getting the person concerned to be frank.

'Far be it from me but I couldn't help seein' that he had nathin' on him,' does not necessarily imply that the individual referred to was going around nude. It conveys simply that the poor chap is badly failed.

'I just stayed in bed till I got up.'

'Keepinwell?' is usually a routine inquiry, normally bringing the 'I'm-not-too-bad' or 'Could-be-worse' response. It should be asked cautiously in Northern Ireland for it is often looked on as a challenge. It is a question not to be put if you are in a hurry.

You are safe if the reply takes the form of 'Ackave bittava edic' or comes in such variations as:

'Ackava wee touch av lambago.'

'Ackava wee whinge in the knee.'

'Ackava a dinge in ma leg.'

The listener has only to murmur sympathetically, 'I'm sorry to hear that,' and all is lost. Everything will come spilling out.

When two health addicts meet head on matters are different. Each has little basic interest in the other's tale of woe but it's a case of having to thole it, and thole it they do.

Nevertheless, some editorial surgery on the torrent of words inspired by the subject of well-being can produce interesting results.

There was this fascinating dialogue outside a health centre:

'I wish ar wee dacter was back from his holidays. The 'tractor dacter talks awful funny. I think he's an Indian.'

'Ack, he's not still there is he? I'm goin' in till see him now. I was in bed with him only last week and he never even tuk my clothes aff. He left me that wake I haven't a leg under me. I hadda walk on m'man's arm or I'd nivver have got this far.'

Everyone understood clearly when a late arrival in the doctor's waiting room said, 'I'm glad to get sitting down for I'm having it all taken out.' She then blew her nose noisily.

A cry of the heart came from a patient brought to Belfast from Dungannon who said, 'It's like this. If I sometimes didnae feel better I wudnae know I wuz as bad as I am.'

A woman with severe stomach pains was offered a stiff whiskey, and told, 'Put that to your head and you'll be as right as rain.'

'But the pain isn't in my head,' came her protest.

A hospital patient learned that the woman in the next bed had been given a sleeping pill and said, 'I could do with one myself.' It was then late afternoon ad she was told that the nurse would be round again at 10.30 that night.

'I was at the end of my tether the way my man was hangin' on the
mantelpiece with his stummick.'

'Ack, sure I could be fast asleep by then.'

Health centre conversations are a constant revelation.

'They're going to operate on a hammer toe that's been giving me gyp for years now.'

'Maybe they'll find a chisel when they do.'

'Ack, nat at all. Sure I had my womb out ages ago.'

One woman confided to the waiting sufferer beside her. 'My man's quaren bad so he is. He has the thyroid glans in his stummick. No wonder he hasn't been well.'

Another confidence ran, 'He heard the doctor say to give him his head and he said "Ye can have it for it's splittin' anyway."'

Doctors are not always unappreciated. 'That wee man that has been seeing to my Albert is just great. Nivver complains. Call him out at four in the morning and he'll say "Missus dear, don't apologise. Doesn't it get me away from the wife for a while?" Mind you, though, I wudden call him at that time if it was snowin'.'

As if making a disclosure of profound importance a woman said, 'I just stayed in bed till I got up.'

Possibly she had a similar complaint to that of the lady who declared, 'I can't work standing up. Only if I'm sitting.'

Fearing that medical attention might be needed an attendant hurried to the help of a woman who left her seat in some agitation during the first act of a church play.

'It's all right,' she said. 'It's just that I wasn't feeling too hot in there for I was far too warm.'

Every hospital, every health centre, every doctor's waiting room has its character, the equivalent of the life and soul of the party.

Like the lady who disclosed to a friend, 'I was going to have my sister-in-law to stay with us for Easter but the doctor told me I wasn't to have any relations for three months so I had to put her off.'

And the casualty arrival who was asked 'How did you come to break your arm?' and solemnly answered, 'I came in a bus.'

An unexpected excuse for failure to keep a health clinic appointment took the form of, 'I wasn't able to make it yesterday. I was at the end of my tether the way my man was hangin' on the mantelpiece with his stummick.'

Certain to win sympathetic audiences were the woman who 'worked her elbow to the bone' and the office cleaner who declared, 'I've just scrubbed my guts out.'

The statement 'He lost his leg in the City' doesn't refer to the absent-minded owner of a wooden leg. The City is one of Belfast's biggest hospitals.

A Visiting Day quote reported from there was: 'I was in Ward Five till they found my legs and then the shifted me to Ward Three.'

'These oul boots are on their last legs.'

There is a constant tendency for limbs to develop a personality of their own in Ulster, a separate existence, a life completely independent of the rest of the body.

It is easy to understand the lament of the shoe shop salesman. He said of a customer who had tried on nearly every pair stocked by the establishment, 'I can't get that woman's feet out of my head.'

She would probably be the type who would lament, 'I can go nowhere with my feet,' and, as a child, told her friend 'I got told aff over the head of a pair of shoes.'

The chemist who was handed a prescription and was asked 'Wud ye send it down. It's my feet, y'know,' clearly understood for he nodded in sympathetic agreement.

Northern Ireland must be a chiropodist's paradise. The air is filled with lamentations relating to the troubles of perambulation.

Two elderly ladies were chatting on a bus and one said, 'I was away down at Tollymore Park in these shoes. They're all right for steppin' out in but they're no use for walkin'.'

A woman told a friend, 'My man had gastric flu that tuk the heels aff him as well as the stiffness outa his legs.' Clearly he didn't know his luck.

Luck didn't come into it in the case of the motorist whose car broke down outside Belfast. He stopped a passing car and asked the driver if he knew anything about car engines.

'I'm not a mechanic at all,' was the reply. 'Actually I'm a chiropodist.'

'In that case,' he was asked, 'could you givvus a tow?'

An elderly Lisburn woman summed up her position by announcing, 'These oul boots av mine are on their last legs.'

'These shoes are too big for me but I can't wear my own with my feet,' said a weary walker.

She sounds like a suitable subject for the admonition: 'If you aren't careful you'll land on your back with your feet.'

'My feet's shippin' water,' has another variation which goes, 'My feet's wringin' wet.'

Footwear salesmen learn to disply sympathetic understanding in all kinds of circumstances. Their days are filled with moving revelations from customers:

'Ack, I wish I was home. It's that hot my shoes are full of feet so they are.'

'It's a funny thing about my husband. Every time he stands up he sits out.'

'I flew to Spain for my holidays but it was terrible warm. My feet kept sticking to me.'

'I got a wee bite on my heel and it got terrible angry.'

'The caretaker at the wee lad's school is a quare geg. He told the wee sowl this morning, "Don't come up them steps with your feet." '

The strange complications involving other parts of the anatomy are no less varied.

This was demonstrated by the woman shopper, struggling with four or five parcels, who told the man who thoughtfully held the shop door open for her, 'Thanks very much, Mister. I've no hauns the day.'

Surprisingly she didn't make the suggestion, 'Could you lennus a haun?' Hand-lending is a common Ulster custom.

The statement will frequently be heard, 'I had one of my heads this morning,' carrying the implication that the first task of the day is to choose which one of them to use.

'Sammy's in bed with his head,' 'That fella has his head screwed on this morning,' and 'That fella has a right head on him' all have implications that the Province is coming down with the hydra-headed.

Even the possession of a single head can produce odd results as in 'I put my head round the door and rapped it' and 'He put his head round the door and shouted, "Yupyit?" '

'I never want a headcahe,' is a characteristically Ulster way of indicating that the speaker is seldom without one.

But physical irregularities don't stop with heads and feet.

The woman who said, 'I have a sore knee and I can't stand on it' could well have been the same person who insisted, 'Aunt Aggie's been kickin'' since her leg caught up with her.'

It may even have been her husband whose legs 'left him in the street last Friday'.

'Wee Agnes has a funny leg and we cudden get to the bottom of it' has its own undertones of mystery, while it is easy to appreciate the fervour of the woman of whom it was said, 'She's that holy she has the knees prayed outa her tights so she has.'

For obvious reasons the invitation, 'We'll go in here and sit down for a minute or two till see how we stand,' is usually extended outside a public house.

'When he came home last night his face was trippin' him,' tells its own story of a husband who is rarely a ray of sunshine.

In a different case the man of the house was referred to in the words, 'Child dear, it's no use waitin' up for yir da for when he does get home he won't be able to bite his finger.'

Yet the world of physical eccentrics is not confined to humans. This is shown by the complaint, 'That dog of theirs is always makin' a haun of the plants in my garden. One of these days I'll show it my boot.'

In danger of distinction

Malapropisms have long been a characteristic of Ulster speech but it would be a mistake to think that their use always arises solely through ignorance of the word in mind. The malapropism should not necessarily be dismissed as the resort of the inarticulate, the refuge of the clueless.

There are times when the impression is created that the device is quite deliberately adopted. More than one malapropism I have heard could earn a place in acceptable contemporary language.

An example comes from a discussion on high prices between two women at the butcher's. One of them summed up the entire economic dilemma in the words: 'It's all this inflammation that's at the bottom of it.'

And there would appear at times to be a fair enough reason for the comment heard at Belfast airport: 'The only way to travel to London is on the scuttle service.'

Condensation is a perpetual stumbling block to Northern Ireland Housing Executive tenants. The word itself has almost been elbowed out of use, if the condition unfortunately remains.

Anything but untypical is the grumble, 'The condencension is drivin' me up the walls. It's that bad I'm catchin' goldfish in the mousetrap.'

Another runs, 'The compensation in the kitchen is terrible. The cooker's bein' ate away with the rust.'

One indignant complainant said, 'I hafta put aero refreshers in every room in the house. You'll have to do something about my decension.'

Another put the blame for much of the trouble on the growing number of 'dialect houses'. Her remedy was 'Demolition them and no more nonsense.'

Summing up the condecension issue, an official made the wry comment:

31

'Hardly anyone now uses the proper word for it. You could almost say it is in danger of distinction.'

The man who had 'crutch courage' and the patient who told her dentist she had 'terrible plague' are not as eccentric as they seem, nor is the lady who insisted that her husband was in need of 'physical therapy'.

A raw new grocery assistant did her best to help when a customer asked if she could have something for her flatulence. 'I'm sorry, missus, we haven't anything that would do but they sell repair kits in the bicycle shop at the corner.'

There is a hysterical sort of logic about the argument: 'This methylated drinkin'. If it was made legal it would overmine the whole thing.'

The swimmer who complained, 'Them baths is unfit for human consumption' underlined his grievance by adding, 'The Council's going to find itself in deep water if something isn't done.'

The comment, 'We had advocates for our dinner but they didn't taste very nice,' implies that it can be a bitter experience to treat the law with less than respect.

It is not outside the bounds of probability that the words were spoken by the woman who said she was looking for a record of 'Mulligan's Tyres' when what she wanted was 'Mull of Kintyre'.

Enter the world of the malapropism and you have to keep your wits about you, as much to grasp the message as the word which should have been used.

'I'm going to get the cat orchestrated,' is not too difficult to interpret, nor is 'The wee girl's learnin' the dismal system' but a moment's thought is needed to catch the sense of 'My man won a computer tankard at the darts.'

The answer by a candidate in a police examination, 'The motorist should be told to expire into the breathalyser' brings implications of its own but there are equally strange undertones about other answers from prospective members of the constabulary:

'Justifiable assault is where there are exterminating circumstances.'

'It is justifiable assault when there are excruciating circumstances.'

'Rape is unlawful cardinal knowledge.'

The mother who announced her determination to buy her daughter 'one of them tripe recorders for her birthday' may not have been as idiotic as she sounded. This could hardly be said of the caravan owner who boasted 'My van has everything. In fact is is fully acquitted.'

A factory personnel officer showed a clear concept of the problem when a workman wanted to know what he could do about his wife because a friend 'was making advantages to her'. The advice given was 'Don't do anything rash.'

Complaining of the starlings which kept invading his garden a house-holder said, 'The other birds never get a crumb. The bread I put out is always gobbled up by the stallions.'

When a sport star's marriage broke up it led to the unexpected comment, 'He would have been wiser if he'd married a more manured women.'

A party of Belfast schoolboys was taken on a soccer trip to the US and during a tour of New York their guide pointed out Harlem.

'We have one in Belfast as well,' a boy exclaimed.

'Where?' he was asked in surprise.

'Sure we have the shipyard — Harlem and Wolff's.'

On a visit to her doctor a Banbridge woman said, 'I hope you'll spare my flushes' and not long after another patient explained, 'It's like this, doctor. I have very close veins.'

Film titles can create their own difficulties. A woman who saw *Spartacus* and obviously enjoyed it said, '*Asparagus* is a great picture'. One interesting revival which drew Belfast crowds was *Gone with the Wine*.

Heard in a Belfast shopping queue was the revelation, 'The doctor sent me to the Royal on my feet but nobody up there knows nothin'. When you ask a civil question they just luck at you.'

'What were you asking?'

'Sure I was only askin' the way to the cherry octopus.'

It is to be hoped she did eventually find the chiropodist.

Notes from parents to teachers are a great source of ill-used words. 'Please excuse Jimmy as I had a baby boy and needed him. Thanks for your corporation.'

Unquestionably a suitable subject for a 'vocal anaesthetic' was the woman who said firmly, 'The Pope's inflammable.'

This could certainly be said of the Portadown woman who confided, 'The child hadda go to hospital for an operation on his wee tentacles.'

'She riz perches so she did.'

'She riz perches so she did.'

Catching up with the metric age continues to pose problems for the older generation. The old conventions linger on. It will be a long time before they are finally dislodged.

'Take Lizzie,' a woman explained to a friend. 'She's that nervous you'd hardly credit it. She was goin' home the orr night there when a big dog jumped outa the hedge and d'y know this? She riz perches so she did.'

It sounds much more dramatic when put like that than saying, 'She jumped several feet in the air.'

Feminine logic takes many forms. A woman who had been shopping wanted to indicate the measure of her success and announced 'I got Harry a new shirt and look till you see what it says on it.'

She indicated in triumph the words 'pure man-made fibres' on the garment and exclaimed, 'None of your oul rubbitch there!'

Belfast's Shankill Road is full of surprise for the eavesdropper.

'When I see her again I won't luk at her. I'll luk through her. I won't even ignore her.' What words could more explicitly sum up a conviction that the individual concerned wasn't all she should have been?

The tenant of a new house in the area, complaining that a cupboard door wouldn't open properly, insisted, 'When I close it it's still half open.'

Later, describing a Spanish holiday, she remarked, 'I was bakin' on the beach the whole day.'

'Did they have a bread strike there too?' her friend asked innocently. More than once bakers in Belfast have been involved in indistrial stoppages.

But the curiosities of speech come in no less profusion from the Falls Road.

One resident summed up the problem of catering for family tastes with, 'My man's the divil for white bread. He has my head turned. Ye cud say he has colour prejice.'

The confession was heard in a supermarket, 'I don't often get out in the wet weather but when I do I get in as much as I can of what I'm out of.'

A woman whose character assassination of a neighbour was summed up·by 'She has awful big shortcomin's' gave short shrift to an insurance agent who called.

As he was passing through the kitchen he observed a large saucepan boiling on the stove and commented hopefully, 'That's a lovely smell. Is that the dinner cooking? It makes my mouth water.'

'Dinner! Man dear that's Jimmy's winter combs. I'm washin' them and they're that thick I'm givin' them a good boil. You'd find them a bit tough.'

It is not wildly unlikely that it was the same woman who told her milkman, 'I couldn't pay you yesterday for I had no teeth in.'

A shopper said to a neighbour, 'Ach but your hair looks awful nice. Where did you get it done?'

'Ach I didn't get it done,' was the reply. 'I just washed it last night in the sink.'

Woodstock Road was the location of the incident involving a young man collecting round the doors for a well-known charity. He was caught in a heavy downpour and a kindly householder offered him the loan of an out-size waterproof.

'I know it'll drown you but it'll keep your dry,' she explained.

This district also housed the woman who boasted to a friend about a sister who had been celebrating because she was seventy. 'I got them to send her Bertie Greetings on the wireless.'

'How did you get your lip cut?' a Crumlin Road resident was asked.

'It was the budgie. I was giving it a bit of bread outa my mouth. Did your budgie ever bite you?'

'Nivver. Our's wudden do that. Ours is wild tame.'

An inquiry about a Bangor man brought the informative reply, 'You'll not find him the day an' forby he starts nights in the mornin'.'

The statement, 'I hadn't on me when he called' is crystal clear to any Ulster hearer but there were puzzled looks from people nearby on a beach in Majorca when an Ulster holidaymaker said in a loud voice to his wife, still wearing a fairly heavy coat, 'Are yet nat takin' aff ye?'

A Belfastman was heard making the dry comment about the factory where he worked, 'Funny place to find myself. One of the bosses is the Invisible Man. There's a notice that says "The Personnel Manager cannot be seen on Thursdays".'

A prospective purchaser took a little time to work out the advice displayed on another notice on one of the walls, 'Do not open front door if the back door isn't shut.'

And there is a compelling quality about the words of the woman who said, 'My man's awful attached to his feet. He's always lukin' after them. One of these days he'll make a bust of them. Mark my words.'

Precision marked this dialogue in a bank queue.

'Cashin' a cheque?' a woman was asked by an acquaintance.

'Am.'

'Soami. A don't come here myself though for this is *his* bank.'

Strength of character was needed to handle the situation involving a heavily-laden woman shopper who went into a drapery store in Cookstown and took a seat in one of the chairs provided for customers.

She distributed her parcels carefully around her, leaned back in relief, and said to the assistant, 'Ye don't mind if I wait here? My bus doesn't come in for a whole half-hour. Sure it doesn't take long to wait for half an hour.'

During a period of heavy snow two women were chatting on the pavement. One was discussing the poor bargain she had made in her choice of husband. Nearby several men were busily clearing the footpath outside their homes.

'Which of them is yir man?' the woman was asked.

'That one there. Him shovellin' the snow with his bare head.'

It could only have been in a Belfast store where a woman buying a mattress pointed to one she liked and asked, 'This tick tuk?'

But it is hardly likely that it was the same lady who was a stickler for having her small son speak more politely than was his wont. She kept trying to steer him away from down-to-earth usages.

One day he came home from school to announce, 'We were learning about Robin Hood this morning. Robin Hood and Friar Tuck.'

'No, Johnny,' said his mother sharply. 'It's took, not tuck.'

'They're only let on bananas.'

Nothing seems to induce the all-revealing remark like the business of going shopping in Ulster. It seems to bring out the spoken word at its most scintillating.

Evidence of this is provided by the woman in the supermarket who was out to make her voice heard. 'Ninety pence a pound for a twenty-pound turkey! I never heard the like. If that bird had only lived to see its carcass hanging up there it would be proud to know it was as dear as a sow twenty years ago.'

It was at a supermarket check-out that a woman was heard to comment to a friend, 'That's a power of groceries you're gettin' for your wee family. They must be quaren fond of the nosebag.'

I have been assured that in one large drapery store the following dialogue is a regular occurence, the only variation being in the garment specified. It provides a fascinating sidelight on feminine deviousness.

'I'm looking for a skirt for myself.'

'What size?'

'I wear a 30-inch waist.'

After studying a selection of garments the customer will say, 'I'll just leave it for now. It's not for myself y'see, so I'll tell her.'

One woman trying on an over-generously cut coat that had obviously reached the bargain rail because it wouldn't fit anybody finally delivered her verdict: 'It's big enough anyway. I'll say that for it. Ye could camp out in it.'

A woman entered a photographic shop with a fairly ancient camera and asked if they could help her. The film had jammed.

Vainly the assistant tried to release it and finally handed it back. 'Know what I'm going to tell you? I would hold on to that camera for dear life for it'll be worth money after a while.'

In a store displaying bowls of articifical fruit a five-year-old rebuked his younger brother, 'Don't touch them, Alfie. They're only let on bananas.'

Requests have interesting variations. One establishment will be asked for 'a pair of strong men's laces'. In another the request will be for 'a pair of black men's socks'.

During a strike which stopped bread supplies a woman asked a friend, 'Is there any bread up your way?'

'For God's sake don't come near the place,' she was told. 'Sure they're atin' one another for it.'

Back came the comment, 'That's terrible. The way I am now I could ate a whole loaf without openin' it.'

In a hardware store a shopper asked if she could have a word with a particular assistant.

'He isn't in yet,' it was explained. 'He'll be wore out this morning. He was cloddin' darts all night.'

An English caravanner could have been more tactful when he visited a shop in Enniskillen and was asked, 'What would you be after?'

'Well I'm just after my lunch but I'd like a pint of paraffin to be going on with.'

Patience is vital to anyone seeking to be a success as a shoe-shop assistant. One of them was sorely tried by a customer who tried on an endless variety of footwear and went off without buying.

'Some other time,' he murmured hopefully as she left, sure he had seen the last of her but determined to hide his feelings.

Next day she returned. He listened in astonishment as she said, 'There's a pair I tried on yesterday, I think I'll take them. I didn't take them yesterday for I was meeting my father-in-law and I didn't want him to think I had money to burn.'

Nostalgia took over in the case of a woman buying groceries: 'God I mind the days when ye could get a quart of lamp oil, a Sedlitz powder, a quarter ounce of snuff, two candles, five Woodbines, a Reckitt's blue and tin of cocoa in yir stride, an' ye didn't need a trolley to put them in.'

An order in a chemist's took the form of, 'Give us some of them tablets you said were good, for you wouldn't know my ma with her head this morning.'

As an example of Israeli humour a Haifa sociologist told of the small boy whose mother directed, 'Go down to the grocer's and see if he had pig's feet...'

The boy returned empty handed. 'I don't know,' he told his mother. 'He had his boots on.'

The sociologist criticised the story, saying that no proper kosher shop would sell pig's feet. When I first heard it the setting was Sandy Row. The arguments are strong that this was where it began. Sandy Row people have no inhibitions about the consumption of pig's feet.

Traders in Ulster wouldn't be long in business if they lacked a sharp ear for the nuances used by customers. They need to know in a flash what is meant when they are faced with such requests as:

'Could I have a wee taste of Ronuk?'

'I want two of yir wee corned loaves.'

'I'm lookin' for a pair of them far away glasses.'

'Hev ye anything that would be good for a gumboil on my hip?'

'I want a suit I can laugh in.'

If Bellymeena is not spelled quite like that on the map, every Ulsterman is familiar with the town and its people. It is fundamental to Ulster folklore. If it had not come into existence because of the number of Scots who settled in the area it would have had to be invented.

A language cult of its own has been produced because of the insistence of the inhabitants in using an 'e' where most people use an 'a' sound.

To stress that they are realists Bellymeena people will tell you they are 'only interested in fex'.

Of a weakling it will be said, 'He lex stamina.'

A shopkeeper will not ask, 'Say that again?' if a customer says she wants 'A pecket of clothes pex.'

On Budget Day the question on every lip in the town is 'What's he goin' to tex nex'?'

A family in trouble will have their 'bex to the wall!'

A harassed mother will lament, 'Them childer — they just won't wash their nex.'

A tirelessly retold story of Bellymeena attitudes concerns the venerable farmer seen disconsolately regarding a field of potatoes, ready for digging.

He is asked why he should be looking so upset and answers gloomily, 'It's the sex.'

'You should have more sense, mon,' he is told. 'You shouldnae be worryin' about a thing like that at your time of life.'

'Of course I should. All them potatoes an' a hinnae onny sex tae put them in.'

The town has a reputation for meanness which hardly seems justified. Prudence rather than stinginess is the watchword.

There is certainly a persistent tendency to haggle. Under no circumstances will a Bellymeena shopper accept that the price quoted is the price really expected, whatever the product.

A woman buying a book of stamps in a local Post Office asked the surprised assistant if they weren't cheaper if bought in bulk.

The town is sometimes made to sound like the centre of Northern Ireland's crank belt. This is to do it an injustice. No such charge could fairly be laid against a place capable of fathering the man who was buying a ready-made suit. He complained that the one offered him was too tight and declared, 'Man dear, I want a suit I can laugh in.'

It could be said that he had something in common with the resident who insisted that he wanted a shirt he could sleep in.

It was a Bellymeena man who was asked, 'How are you getting on?' and replied, 'Rightly if I cud onny cut my toenails.'

The ladies are no less quotable. A woman said to a friend, 'That was a powerful bit of a coat Eileen had on last Sunday.'

'Wasn't it now. I thawat the ventilator at the beck gey set it aff.'

Extravagance is frowned on, even if it involves holidays. 'We're not plannin' on havin' any holidays this year. The prices they're charging! We're just going for a day here and a day there but I'm telling you the way things are it'll more often be a day here.'

The town would have its own contribution to make to a controversy in the correspondence columns of a national newspaper over the negative form of 'Scots wha hae'.

No argument about it, they would say, taking it completely out of Scottish hands. 'It's Scots wha haeney'.

The expression figures in the frequently used phrase, 'A haeney onny change.' Running it close are, 'Ye haeney bocht me a drink this lang while,' and 'Ye wudney hae a match on ye?'

It was a farmer in the district who stopped his horse and cart on a narrow road that had a deep sheugh running alongside, and waited for a friend to open a gate for him.

A motorist was approaching at a fast speed and the farmer roared, 'Whoa there. Ye'll whammel the kert if ye don't watch.'

Ask a resident the time of day and you could be left in some confusion if you're a stranger.

If it is eight-thirty you'll be informed, 'It's heff eiate.' Should it be one-thirty you'll be told, 'It's heff yin.'

Where in Belfast you'll learn 'It's two a'clack' in Bellymeena it is 'Two a'clawk.'

Anyone lacking the townspeople's bilingual qualities would find difficulty in appreciating that a tribute was being paid to the excellent organ in Belfast Cathedral by the Bellymeena man who went with a friend to one of the services.

'Weel, did ye like it?' his companion asked.

'Aye I was o'er fond of it. The Psalms were guid but I was fair taken wi' thon chest of whostles.'

It is said that since 1629 more than ninety-six languages have been invented, ranging from Solresol to Esperanto and Suma. A visit to Bellymeena would give the impression that the native tongue used there is yet another one.

Take the two men travelling to the town on a crowded train. One has a parcel containing two pairs of shoes he had bought at a bargain price at a summer sale.

His companion pointed to the luggage rack and said, 'Willie John, why don't ye put your sheen on the shelf?'

From nowhere else in the Province could come the story of the cautious admirer who had his own way of paying unobtrusive visits to his lady friend.

'He didnae gae from his to hers as the crow flies but changed the route by gan from his tae there, then tae there, there tae there, and so on, but always getting to hers frae a different there. Och but sure he was the talk of the place. Everybody knew where he was gan anyway.'

It could only in in Bellymeena that a small boy would go into a shop and say, 'M'ma sent me for a hard tamata.'

According to the saying, 'You can tell a Bellymeena man anywhere but you can't tell him much.'

But it is also put about that, 'If he comes from Bellymeena he's no goat's toe.' Could there be a nicer compliment?

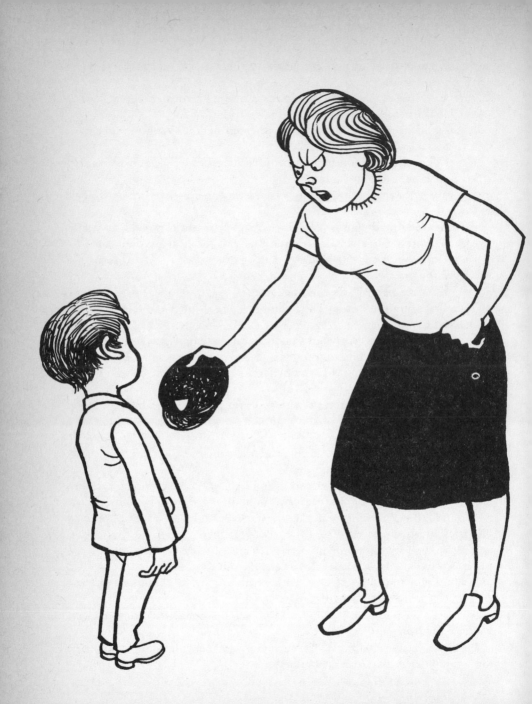

'Put that cap on this minute or I'll knock the head aff ye.'

'Do you want to feel the weight of my hand?'

Mother and child relationships, as reflected in their family speech patterns, offer a revealing aspect of the Ulster way with words.

When addressing their children, mothers tend towards hyperbole, especially if a reprimand is being delivered.

Usually, however, parental threats are not intended to be taken seriously. The menace often lies more in the manner of delivery than in the actual words. The more violent the threat the greater the extent to which it conceals depths of affectionate concern.

Children tend naturally to communicate in the manner used by their parents but while youngsters don't address to each other the growls directed at them, they will frequently seek to emulate the style.

Playground battles can be won or lost solely because of the colourful quality of the threats that fill the air. An imaginative mum generally has a child not far behind her in verbal agression.

Violence is mainly of the mind in the parental censure, 'I'll twist the arm aff ye if you don't stop drivin' me out of my mind with yir whingin'.'

A mother's dire warning, 'Come cryin' home to me with another bleedin' knee and I'll murder ye', can actually conceal the deepest affection.

Similarly there would be an indignant denial that anything other than mother love was indicated by 'Put that cap on this minute or I'll knock the head aff ye.'

'Do you want to feel the weight of my hand?' is not intended as a serious invitation. It is merely a reflection of impatience liable to lead to more painful consequences.

Ears are constantly in the picture when the target for a reprimand is specified. There is the indication of disapproval which runs, 'I'm goin' to warm your ear for you,' or 'Are you lookin' for a right bat along the lug?'

A common style of admonition is 'If you utter another word I'll smart the back of your ear.' Others run:

'I'll box your ears till they ring for a week.'

'If you don't stop your fidgetin' I'll pull your ears till they're as long as an ass's.'

'If I hear another cheep outa you I'll give you a skite across the lug.'

'Yir lookin' for a clip on the ear, aren't you?'

'I'll warm your behind for you' introduces another part of the anatomy which figures regularly in disciplinary reference.

The stern warning, 'You won't sit down for a week after I've finished with you' usually has the desired effect.

So too has 'If you don't sit still you'll get a skelp on the behind you'll mind for a fortnight.'

One harassed mother delivered the admonition, 'If it was any other day of the week but Friday I'd ate you for what you've done, you wee ruffian.'

The trouble with all these threats, of course, is that they can only be effective if used infrequently. It is important to keep ringing the changes if displeasure is to be effectively indicated.

The all-embracing indictment, 'You're a wee girner, you were a wee girner from the day you were born, and you'll be a wee girner till the time you die' has a well-defined sweep.

So too have 'If you don't eat your dinner you'll lick where it lay,' and 'Will you behave yourself before I get your teeth pulled and put you back on the breast?'

All are useful Ulster alternatives to the milder indications of disfavour covered by 'Behave yourself or I'll not speak to you again.'

Children to whom the more exaggerated threats are part of the process of growing up have a fair idea that the more frightening the punishment conjured up, the less likely is the prospect of its imposition.

Picturesque but hardly feasible is the warning, 'If you don't do what you're told I'll stick you up on the wall and only bring you down when I need you.'

It is in the same class as 'Take anything more that doesn't belong to you and it won't be the police I'll send for. It'll be the bloody ambulance.'

Much more effective than the conventional 'I'll have to speak to your da about ye,' is 'If you don't quit your nonsense you'll find you'll be as long as a barber's pole after I've done with you.'

A mother will try anything to induce discipline.

The Belfast soccer side known as the Whites has good seasons and bad. During one of their less successful periods a youngster was threatened: 'If you don't behave I'll make you go and watch the Whites with yir da so I will.'

A cry of despair in another case of misbehaviour was 'Every time I look at ye all that happens is that ye mind me of your da and he's worse than the toothache.'

There is a world of menace in the threat of one parent at the end of her tether: 'The next time you tear the sate outa yir trousers you'll be sent to school in your granny's bloomers, and see how you like that!'

But mother and child relationships aren't always bitter. One of the more pleasant moments was put like this: 'He's a dear wee lad. You wanta see him skellying. His morr has a skelly, y'know, and the wee sowl copies her.'

'The opposite of "sober" is "full".'

It could be that the language used by Ulster mothers has something to do with it, but youngsters are far from routine in the things they say.

An 11-plus candidate, confronted with the question 'What is the opposite of sober?' solemnly answered, 'Full'. It is to be hoped he got full marks.

A teacher read to her class the line, 'A mouse in the wainscot was scratching and scratching,' and asked if anyone knew what a wainscot was.

'Please miss, a baby's cradle,' was the instant answer.

The boy who insisted that 'Brian Boru drove the dames out of Ireland' had his own concept of history but it took a long time for one small boy to realise his error when instructed, 'Go over the road and ask how old Mrs Young is.' She had been ill for several days.

The lad did as was told, literally, and came back with the answer, 'She said to tell you it's none of your business how old she is.'

A little girl went running home to say she had something in her eye. She was told to blow her nose vigorously and it would go away.

'But I want to keep my nose,' she objected. 'It's the thing in my eye I want out.'

Parents seem to fight a losing battle in their efforts to hammer home the correct use of English. In a farming area a youngster ran home with the news, 'Morr, the yo has lambed.'

'Not yo,' he was told. 'Yew.'

'Not me, morr,' said the child. 'The yo.'

A visiting school inspector had the feet taken from under him when he sought to try out a class in the heart of a farming area.

He pinned an enlarged picture of a sheep on the blackboard and asked what it was. He was met by a wall of silence.

'Come,' he said, 'Surely country children should be able to tell me.'

There was still no response and he finally pointed to one youngster and asked him to take a good look.

Carefully the boy studied the picture, pondered for a moment or two, then said, 'Ah'm no sure but Ah think it's a twa-year-old Border Leicester.'

The same class had been told to memorise a portion of the 23rd Psalm. One pupil came up with this version of one of the lines, 'Surely to goodness mercy will follow me all the days of my life.'

And credited to the same school is the reply given by a boy angler who was asked what he was catching.

'Fash,' he replied curtly.

Possibly he was still smarting from his mother's threat, caused by her irritation at the rough usage he had given his new footwear, 'The next pair of shoes you'll get will be a pair of boots.'

Reasons given by parents for school absences give a fascinating insight into the ailments which keep children at home.

One mother wrote, 'Please excuse Tommy the day. He has a cowpy stummick, a beelin' heel, an' a sore nose an' can't luk outa his eyes.'

Stummick troubles are far from infrequent. School records tell of Jimmy who 'vomited up the Woodstock Road,' Ronald who 'vomited up the Crumlin Road,' and Geordie, who 'vomited up the Portrush Road.' There was also Sammy who was kept at home because he 'vomited up the Ormeau Road.'

Cissie's case was different. She 'vomited up the back loanin'.'

Wee Shuey was an odd man out. He was 'taken over with quareness and when he was coming home for his dinner be boked up Barrack Hill.'

Sally couldn't make it to the classroom either. 'She has a pane in her eye and can't see through it.'

Another example of juvenile distress was described in the words, 'Please excuse our Jamesie. He was sick and throwin' up and it went over all the rest of the family.'

Albert had a different excuse. His worried mother wrote, 'Please forgive him being aff all last week. I needed him to help me as I had a wee baby and it wasn't his fault.'

Absenteeism takes many forms. One note to a teacher said, 'Sorry Sandra was off again. I can't get her to go on a Thursday for she's afeered of Jim.'

Which was another way of indicating that the child dreaded coming a cropper in the gym class.

Another note ran, 'I'm sorry Johnny was absent but I'm carrying and expected delivery of a twin pram so I kept him at home to help me but the man never came.'

Parental notes are rarely dull. Among the many other gems are:

'My wee lad has been billious all night and won't be there. His head is affected but he hopes to shake it off as soon as possible.'

'The child won't be at school the day for he has diarhea and as his boots are lettin' in it'll be a day or two before he sees yous.'

After the death of the last Pope a twelve-year-old was heard to comment, 'But sure they can always get another Pope. We can't get another King William.'

It is an outlook not unlike that reflected by the child whose bedside prayer ran, 'God bless Mummy and God bless Daddy and keep him out of the frying pan.'

Asked by her bewildered father what she meant she explained, 'Mummy says you drink like a fish and fish are fried in the pan, aren't they?'

'He died with all his facilities.'

Anyone who finds himself among the mourners at a Northern Ireland wake can depend on it that the occasion will not be marked by deafening silence. A funeral is looked on as a time for talking, not for hush.

The tributes to the deceased take many forms, as in, 'If he ever did anybody any harm it was himself. If he had a bad head you would never know he had it.'

'When they said he was gone it was such a shock my eyes never met for hours.'

'There's one thing about him. He died with all his facilities.'

'Sudden? I would hardly say it was all that sudden. Sure he was well into injury time.'

'He was a terrible man for complaining. He was a cratur who always had the wind in his face and never at his back.'

A visitor in one house of mourning listened as it was said of the deceased, 'He was a better man than his brother. "Oul' stap the clack." That's what they used to call the brother.'

'Why would that be?' he whispered.

'It's like this. You being a stranger cudden know. When anybody dies all the clocks in the house are stopped. They aren't started again till after the funeral.'

'The brother never had good health,' it was added. 'He was always at death's door and always getting better. It happened that often that's what they called him.'

Commenting on the neglected state of the graveyard which the cortege passed the visitor said it looked quite abandoned.

'Right enough,' came the explanation, 'but then sure there hasn't been a livin' soul buried there for the last twenty-five years.'

Mourning customs survive in country districts in many forms.

'Has somebody told the pigs?' will be asked if death strikes the head of the house. This is because tradition directs that the pigs should be solemnly informed or they won't thrive.

In some areas the news is also conveyed to the hens to ensure that the supply of eggs will not be affected.

It was said of the bereaved wife of a farmer, 'She's that mean she told the oul' rooster twice about it.'

A pensioner, asked at a wake if he would like to live to be a hundred, replied, 'If I thought I was going to be crabbit with it I'd rather go in my nineties.'

A widow had this sombre comment to make to the mourners, 'Ach sure I knew he was going. Once ye hear the rattle in his thrapple ye may give up hopin'.'

Two women who were among those demonstrating their sympathy were asked if they would like a cup of tea.

'No thanks,' one said as her companion nodded in agreement. 'We never drink wake tea.' The probability is that they had their sights on something rather stronger.

Potted obituaries take many forms:

'Sure he went like snow aff a ditch.'

'Mind you I think he'll be a light lift for four.'

'It'll be a powerful funeral. Them flires is awful nice.'

'It was that sudden. I went up till see him last night and I knew right away. An' d'ye know this? His wife didn't wait for him to stiffen till she had a notice saying "House private" on the latch of the door.'

The statement, 'He should have died a month ago,' should not be taken as an indication that the life span of the deceased had been unnecessarily lengthy. It reflects only that the man had been at death's door but miraculously recovered.

At one wake a mourner asked an acquaintance how his ailing brother was keeping.

'Very poorly,' it was explained. 'It's a good thing his mother's dead for if she could see him as he is now it would be the end of her.'

A death is not necessarily an occasion for grief. Often it will be looked on as a good excuse for a party. The rule is that there should be plenty of food and drink, particularly in farming districts.

A wet day is always considered ideal for a burial. The only possible grounds for this is the saying, 'Happy the bride the sun shines on. Happy the corpse the rain falls on.'

But then customs of any kind often have a fairly slender basis.

Discussing the burial of followers of differing beliefs alongside each other rather than in strictly denominational graveyards, a woman asked a friend what she thought of the practice.

'Sure it can do nothing but good,' was the reply. 'It helps to bring people together, after all, and that's what we want.'

But large cemeteries can make for confusion.

A couple had spent some time vainly searching in one of them for the grave of a friend, buried only a short time before. Finally they were directed to the caretaker's house.

As they trudged towards it one of the woman said, 'Edgar must be having the quare laugh at us not being able to find his grave.'

An odd note was also struck, in a sense, when a church organist collapsed and died in the middle of a service. Two women were discussing the incident.

'How did it happen?' one asked.

'The minister told me he had a stroke.'

'Did he tell you that?' said the questioner and instantly sped off in a state of some agitation to spread the news.

'The organist's dead,' she told the first woman she met. 'Didn't you hear?'

'No. Tell us what happened?'

'He cut his throat.'

'Cud I hev some waddan fir meers?'

Put an ear to the ground in Northern Ireland and it will soon be found that, if in showbiz it isn't what you do it's the way that you do it, in Ulster it isn't so much what you say as *how* you say it. While this may be a comment that can be made of other areas it applies with particular force to Norn Irish speakers.

Many of them seem to regard words as playthings, instruments to be treated lightly. Dictionary definitions are considered of no consequence. It is a factor which constantly emphasises the inadequacies of the printed word compared to the spoken word in conveying precisely what a speaker means.

In print, the simple acknowledgment 'Thank you' seems to have one meaning only. Yet a Belfastman can utter 'Thank you' in a manner which can convey a sarcastic 'Thank you for nothing'. 'Thank you very much' can be even more biting, depending on the tone.

'I'm greatly obliged' can have the same variations. It can often take an acute sense of hearing to realise that what is meant is 'I'd be glad if you would mind your own bloody business'.

'I saw you last night' can be heavy with implications that you were somewhere you shouldn't have been at all. 'You're in great form, aren't you?' can hint strongly that there are highly suspicious reasons for your rapture.

'He's a character' can affirm that the gentleman is someone to be admired or that he is utterly unreliable, someone to be carefully avoided, certainly not a man to be trusted. It calls for a degree of shrewdness to spot the meaning really intended.

Radio interviewers are particularly prone to fall into the trap of using word-play all too readily.

An inventor, explaining a new device, will be asked, 'Do you think it will work?' A manufacturer making claims for a new product will have the question put to him: 'Do you think the public will rush to buy it?'

Someone putting forward a new solution to a social problem will be challenged: 'Do you honestly believe it is a good idea?'

All are questions that can be asked with an air of genuine examination, or put in tones of utter disbelief. In print they look completely innocent.

But when the enquiry is made 'Do you think it will work?' all the questioner need do is to utter the word 'work' a note higher than the rest of the sentence and the whole sense is changed. So too with the other questions. Raise the tone just a shade at the end of the query and it is a challenge as distinct from a quiet question.

Ulster speech is impregnated with this approach and careful watch has to be kept to be able to spot it and take the necessary precautions.

'Yir hevin' me on,' for example, can convey: (a) 'You're altogether too flattering to be really sincere,' (b) 'You're pulling my leg, aren't you?,' (c) 'You seem to think I came in on a load of hay,' (d) 'You're joking.'

Those who make the wrong choice lose face. You need to be at least a fourth-year student of Morr tung to understand the correct meaning right away.

'Whaddya take me fir?' posts the question, 'Do I look stupid?' — nothing more or less.

But 'Catch yerself on' can have such implications as: 'You're sailing close to the wind; watch out,' 'One more word and you'll find yourself on your back,' or nothing more than a tolerant, 'Take it easy'.

There are other vernacular conventions which call for local knowledge if they are to be survived unscathed.

The Ulsterwoman on holiday in Majorca who was asked by a member of a French group lounging close by on the sun-drenched beach 'Parlez vous Francais?' and replied, 'A wee bit,' left the inquirer in utter confusion.

He couldn't possibly have known that 'a wee bit' can have a variety of meanings.

'A wee bit down the road' can mean half a mile, and just as readily three miles. 'A wee bit of a laugh' can indicate a mild chuckle or a side-splitting evening of fun. 'A wee bit of a girl' can mean a quiet little maiden or someone pretending to be something she isn't.

It therefore calls for a nice sense of judgment to decide which can cause the greater perplexity — the *way* something is said or *how* it is said.

It is difficult not to feel sympathy for the visitor shopping in Belfast who was told by someone anxious to get past her, 'Pudden me'.

Or for the same stranger who heard the request in a chemist's: 'Cud I hev some waddan fir meers?'

And then had to listen to the enquiry in a china shop, 'Mucher them tummellers?'

Followed by the same devotee of the Queen's English saying, 'The wee lad's gettin' more like his farr's side of the house every day.'

Nevertheless it should be remembered that Ulster people are not exceptional in adding complications to the spoken word.

Consider this test, designed to establish in Yorkshire whether you are an immigrant or a native.

Those able to give the translations in 30 seconds were considered to be local inhabitants. Those who took longer were clearly foreigners.

1. Intitot?
2. Guisit.
3. Summatsupeer.
4. Eez goinome.
5. Astha gorrit reight?
6. Shut thigob.
7. Owzeeno?
8. It dunt marrer.
9. Tintintin.
10. Eenoze nowt abartit.
11. Eez gorrageroff.
12. Azegeniter?

For the benefit of those who put themselves to the test, here are the Morr tung Ulster translations.

1. Sot, innit?
2. Gimme it.
3. Sumthinsupeer.
4. Ees feraff.
5. Didye gettit rite?
6. Shut yir bake.
7. Howdis heno?
8. Dussen marr.
9. Snottin the tin.
10. Henose nathin.
11. Hesgotta gitaff.
12. Asee ginnit ter?

Which rather goes to show that it calls for a sharp ear to achieve star rating when it comes to word power in Ulster.

The 'wee corner shap'.

Corn plasters and gas mantles

Although change has had its inevitable effect on many elements of Ulster's way of going, old customs linger, expressions long in use refuse to take their departure, habits of a lifetime stick.

Fighting hard against the relentless march of time is the 'wee corner shap'. Supermarkets have dealt an ever-increasing number of them a mortal blow but they doggedly continue to provide a useful service — and a place for people to meet, a rostrum for talk and gossip, somewhere to keep abreast of what's going on, to 'hear the latest'.

Many have found their own answer to the competition of the Goliaths. Some have taken to opening from around seven a.m. till nine a.m., then closing till five p.m. and opening for the rest of the evening. Their message is a determined, 'We serve you when the supermarkets don't.'

Owners of wee shaps are a class apart. Frequently the proprietor is a widow or widower, often in business as much for 'the crack' as to supplement a pension. The chance of using one as a path to fortune is remote.

The bankruptcy rate in the business is high, generally because credit is all too easily given. To own one means you rarely take a holiday. The cost in lost business is too steep.

The spirit of enterprise is not completely dormant just because a rush of three or four customers all at once means there isn't room to move.

Corner emporiums tend to become known by the name of the proprietor. 'I'm away to Mrs Crosby's.' 'I'm taking a skite down to Graham's.' 'I'll be at Mrs Mannis's if anybody wants me.' 'I'll only be a tick. I'm taking a wee dart over to McGrew's.' All indicate in their respective areas that the speaker has gone shopping.

In a way each stands for the local equivalent of Fortnum and Mason's.

It is interesting to study an imaginary Mrs McCluggage as typifying the Belfast small shop entrepreneur. What happens in Mrs McCluggage's reflects the entire wee shap routine.

At one stage, because the bell attached to the glass door was proving unreliable, she made it known that she had decided to add a parrot to her labour force of one. The idea was to use the parrot to warn that a customer was waiting.

One report said that she was first offered, cheap, a bird that could speak two languages. In fact its vocabulary consisted of two words — 'Hesferaff,' and 'Good night.'

A lot of people insisted that the whole object was to get the shop talked about. If this is so Mrs McCluggage was demonstrating a considerable talent for publicity.

A bird having been chosen, she persuaded her brother-in-law to take it in hand and it underwent a process of training in the technique of calling out 'Shap!' when a customer appeared.

It was named Abraham because the brother-in-law was religious, according to some residents.

Considered to be purely apocryphal is the suggestion that before long Abraham picked up an additional phrase because from the day of its arrival behind the counter the bell behaved impeccably.

Besides 'Shap!' it was reputed to say quite distinctly, 'Bugger the bell.'

Few Ulstermen are without happy childhood memories of the delights offered by emporiums like Mrs McCluggage's. When today's children are grown-ups they will think nostalgically of the sweets alluringly on show for the benefit of the check-out queues.

Today's adults, however, would never concede that these could really compare with the kali suckers, liquorice bootlaces, sweetie mice, gold mines, Jap nuggets, aniseed balls, lucky dips and all the other tempting confections on offer at Mrs McCluggage's.

Not even the cargoes catalogued in Masefield's poem, 'apes and peacocks, sandalwood, cedarwood and sweet white wine,' had more infinite variety.

Mrs McCluggage, a lamplighter's widow, played a significant part in the lives of those housed in the adjoining streets.

'Sure the truth is that in a wee shap yir helpin' people,' was how she put it. 'Them that keep runnin' outa things at the last minute — they wudden know where to turn. If a woman finds she has no eggs for her man's tea she'd be in the quare pickle if she hadn't the wee shap to run till. Life wudden be worth livin' if there was no wee shap. Many's the time I've heard that said.

'There's one thing. Ye hafta be able to put your finger on the ones that won't pay. After a while yir able to smell them.

'An' ye hafta have a memory like a hawk. Ye have to mine where things are. In two shakes of a lamb's tail I'm able to put my haun' on things like corn plasters an' van Houten's cocoa, chocolate drops an' gas mantles, lead pencils an' shelled peas.

'For a while there I was of a mind to take the house next door and expandin' like but then I thought it wouldn't be worth all the bother.

'I mine the day the childer used to come crowdin' in wantin' to know how much were the hepney mice in the winda. It's not the same now.

'Only last week there I was selling a wee lad an onion. I weighed it on the scales and told him there was 10p in it. The wee fella paid for it and ran home all excited. They tole me afterwards he said to his granny, 'Wud ye cut that open quick. There's 10p in it.''

'One time I was wakened outa my bed at two o'clack in the mornin'. It was a man from the next street. A bittava noddity. He said he wanted a packet of starch, an ounce of snuff, a darnin' needle and a pair of size ten insoles.

'When ye have a wee shap ye meet them all.

I'll never forget the wee woman who ast me for curn jam without the curns in it. It took me a while to find out she wanted black currant jelly.

'An' I mine the woman who took a long look at the dulse an' ast me "Is that dulse false?"

'There's a fren' who turned her parlour intil a wee shap. She tells me she's doin' all right. I said it was fine so long as the customers didn't do the doin'. There was a man who once went in an' said "That's a quare nice smell comin' from the kitchen? Is yir man fryin'?"

'Ye nivver know what people will look for next. A wee woman ast me for a quarter of pickled tea. I lucked at her an' she toul me why. "We're havin' a party," she said, "and a woman in till read the cups. Ordinary tea's nat the same."

'A strange clergyman walked in one day an' lo an' behold he was lookin' for throat lozenges because he was goin' till a weddin' an' forgot them. He said he needed them special for the bridegroom was seventy-eight an' hard av hearin'. "I'll hev to shout myself hoarse at the oul ijit," he said.

'I cud tell ye about the man smokin' a big cigar and drivin' a fancy motor who wanted a packet of notepaper an' a jar of vaseline and wudden take the change out av a poun' note. "Yir very obligin'," he said. "I'll take a pair of brown shoelaces while I'm here."'

Mrs McCluggage nodded contentedly at the memory.

'Once ye hev a wee shap ye wudden be without it. Ye hev a standin'. It's a livin' and forby it passes the time. I'm as happy as Larry behine the counter listenin' to people.'

When the last wee shap closes its doors, the Mrs McCluggages have vanished, and the stocks of nibs and tin tacks, copying ink pencils and strong twine have disintegrated, a social milestone will have been passed.

Glossary

This is designed to act as a help for the ill-informed who may find difficulty with some of the expressions used throughout this book.

A BLAKA RIBBEL	A block of ripple ice cream.
A HINNEY ONNY SEX	'My supplies of sacks are exhausted.' Sometimes 'haenae' is used.
ANORN	Another one; the same again.
ASSE LEF	'Has he taken his departure?' or 'Has he gone?'
AWAY WITH THE BAND	An old illness has struck again. Can also imply pregnancy; up the chute.
BAKE	Mouth. 'I'll draw my haun' across yir bake.'
BARE CHEWS	Pair of shoes.
BERTIE GREETINGS	Birthday greetings. 'We're having a bertie party.'
BIASABUNMA	'Buy me a bun, mother.'
CALLUSTATE	'Call me at eight o'clock.'
CAR DOOR	Carrowdore. 'I come from Car Door.'
CHEST O' WHOSTLES	Church organ.
CLODDIN'	Throwing. 'He was cloddin' stones.'
CLOTHES PEX	Clothes pegs.
COLOUR PREJICE	Colour prejudice. 'My man will ate nathin' but white bread.'
CORNED	Currant. 'I want a corned loaf.'
COWL SWATE	Cold sweat.
CRYIN' BUCKETS	Crying bitterly.

CUMMEERAWANTYE	'Would you come in now?'
DAY MARE	Daily Mirror.
DIRT BIRD	Person of no consequence.
DIALECT HOUSES	Derelict houses; awaiting demolition.
DEADLY CRACK	Considerable fun; an amusing way to pass the time.
FASH	Fish. 'What are you tring to catch?' 'Fash.'
FLIRES	Flowers. 'The flires is lovely.'
FREW DUNT	'For a whodunnit.' 'I'm going to the libery frew dunt.'
GAN	Going. 'I'm gan.'
GAWN YOWLCODYE	'You're pulling my leg.'
GIVEMISJEW	Give him his due. He could be a lot worse.
GLUNTERPAKE	Stupid person.
HASN'T AN OUNCE	Someone who behaves irresponsibly; a scatterbrain.
HEART AND A HALF	Willingly. 'I'll do it with a heart and a half.'
HEFF EIATE	Half-past eight.
HEFF YIN	Half past one.
HEPNEY	Halfpenny.
INFLAMMATION	Inflation. 'It's terrible what inflammation's doing to the price of drink.'
JINNOMABROR	'Do you know my brother?'
LET-ON BANANAS	Imitation fruit.
LIAR INTIT	'Eat it up.' 'Leather into it.'
LOANIN'	Narrow country lane.
MON MOAN	Alone; unaccompanied. 'I'm mon moan since yesterday.'
MUSHERE LUKIN?	'How much do you want?' 'What is your lowest price?'

NAAWALNAT	'No, I will not.' 'I refuse absolutely.'
NAMMEL JUG	Jug made of enamel.
PARRITCH	Porridge
RAMALGERRIES	Band of idiots; collection of incompetents; a choir with tone deaf tenors.
RIZ PERCHES	Jumped several feet in the air.
SACAR	'That's a car.'
SAGES	A long time. 'Sages since I saw a tram.'
SANASS	'That's a donkey.'
SAUCE	Saws. 'He's in the timber business and knows good sauce from bad ones.'
SAVAN	Seven. 'He tuk a savan at the savanth hole.'
SAWN	'It's on,' indicates that it has started raining.
SCOTS WHA HAENEY	Bellymeena's version of Scots wha hae.
SHIZ AWED	She acts extremely oddly; said of a person whose behaviour is unpredictable.
SHIZZENT	'She is not.'
SIN HERE	'It is in here; this is the shop I was talking about.'
SKITE	Blow; dash. 'I'll give you a skite across the gub,' and 'I'm takin' a wee skite down till the shap.'
SOAM	'So I am;' indicates resolve.
SOFT SHOE SHUFFLE	Dance; conventional ballroom waltz or foxtrot.
SODAYI	'So do I.'
WEESHIRE	'It is only a small shower; it's nothing to worry about.'
SPOARIN'	'It is only me.'
SPORIN	'It is pouring.'
SQUARENDEER	'It is very expensive.' 'It is much more costly than I anticipated.'
STAKEN SHIPS	Steak and chips.
STEEMIN	'It is raining fairly heavily.'

TRACTER DACTER	Member of medical team in attendance or on call at a health centre.
THOWLANTS	The old aunts.
THOWLBECK	Phrase used by constant victim of back trouble.
THOWLFEET	Used by person who is in regular need of a chiropodist.
THROWIN' UP	Vomiting.
TWO SHUPPERS	Indicates a desire for two fish suppers to carry out.
TURTLE	Thread hanging down from a dress.
WASSUP?	"What has happened?"
WANCE	Just on one occasion. 'It happened oney the wance.'
WEE KNOWIN'	Small amount.
WEEL GUP NI	'We will now go upstairs.'
WHINGE	Pain. 'I have a wee whinge in my knee.'
WHOP	Whip.
WHAMMEL	Hit, damage or upset. 'Watch or ye'll whammel the kert.'